We are glad to be able to announce a new edition of one of the most important books on the modern movement in architecture.

'Professor Gropius', said the *Spectator* when *The New Architecture and the Bauhaus* first appeared, is the only architect who has attempted a practical solution of the fundamental problems presented by the new relations of art and industry. His new book is an exposition, in extraordinarily simple and lucid form, of the origin and results of this experiment. . . . The book is admirably produced and has a brilliant photomontage jacket by Professor Moholy-Nagy.

'A creed of absolute integrity, clarifying the vital problem of how the architect can regain his proper status of purveyor of an essential service to the community.'—*Architectural Review*

'The lucid text and the brilliance of the accompanying photographs make it an ideal handbook of contemporary architecture.'—*Time and Tide*

'An important book, because Dr. Gropius understands the nature of the modern movement better than any man alive.'—*Architect and Building News*

'Full of important suggestions . . . not only a book for architects. It is a book that everyone can read . . . it has something to say that will make even an architectural student sit up.'—John Betjeman in the *New Statesman and Nation*

The New Architecture
and the Bauhaus

The New Architecture and the Bauhaus

by
Walter Gropius

translated from the German by
P. Morton Shand
with an introduction by
Frank Pick

CHARLES T. BRANFORD COMPANY
Boston, Massachusetts

Printed in Great Britain

Introduction by Frank Pick

Dr. Gropius has asked me to write an introduction to this essay. There seems little need for one. It is a plea for thinking out afresh all the problems of building in terms of current materials and of current tools, tools which have become elaborated into machines. It asks that what the past did for wood and brick and stone, the present shall do for steel and concrete and glass. It rightly claims that only out of such a fresh input of thought can a true architecture be established. What interests me still more, it proceeds to observe that what applies to architecture equally applies in those fields of design which relate to things of everyday use.

Such a plea comes at an opportune time, for a lively attention is being directed by more and more people to these problems. This generation is becoming conscious of art not as something apart and curious, but as something vital and essential to the fullest life, as something which will restore grace and order to society. It is a period of pause in expectation of some renascence of art of which the premonitory symptoms grow more numerous and distinct with each year. I am hopeful in my lifetime of enjoying some measure of its realization. Dr. Gropius has been a pioneer of this movement. He has through the Bauhaus made a decisive contribution to its realization. This country may count itself fortunate in being able to entertain him in this period of transition and to secure his guidance. It might even seek to utilize his knowledge and ability in accelerating the changes that must come, not only in architecture itself, but even more in the teaching of architecture and of art in its widest acceptation.

Dr. Gropius rightly points out that the 'new architecture' begins by being stark and formal, and seeks norms or standards. This is a reaction from the welter of copying and adaptation of styles which have ceased to have significance in relation to modern building. But this reaction has almost spent itself, and the new architecture is passing from a negative phase to a positive phase seeking to speak not only through what it omits or discards, but much more through what it conceives and invents. Individual imagination and fancy will more and more take possession of the technical resources of the new architecture, of its spatial harmonies, of its fit functional qualities, and will use them as the ground work, or rather framework, of a new beauty which will crown this expected renascence with splendour. If the architect has in the reaction swung too far over towards the engineer he will, in the counterreaction, swing back again towards the artist. Progress flows from this wavelike motion. The creative spirit is ever resurgent. The tide relentlessly rises over breaking and receding waves. It is the rise of the tide that matters most.

Let me revert again from the architecture of buildings to suggest that there is some corresponding art, or science, or combination of both, relating to things. If things are to be rightly conceived and executed and to attract to themselves aesthetic qualities, then out of the technical and craft schools dealing with now this, now that thing, some overriding educational discipline and understanding must arise which will do for things what the new architecture will do for building. I could wish

9

that Dr. Gropius had developed the hints and suggestions in his essay on this subject. It is a critical study for this moment. At one time I thought that maybe architects had limited the scope of their training too narrowly in relating it to building, especially whan I saw them venturing into other fields of design such as furniture, decoration, pottery and so forth, but I see now that I was not right. The designer for industry must be placed alongside the architect, with a training equivalent in character, if directed towards another end, and with a status and authority equivalent too. Dr. Gropius must help to define this training and to explore its methods, once more repeating the experiments of the Bauhaus, with architecture as a mistress art certainly, but also with a new architectonic arising out of a collective understanding of design in industry.

Contents

Illustrations

13

15

The New Architecture
and the Bauhaus

Can the real nature and significance of the New Architecture be conveyed in words? If I am to attempt to answer this question it must needs be in the form of an analysis of my own work, my own thoughts and discoveries. I hope, therefore, that a short account of my personal evolution as an architect will enable the reader to discern its basic characteristics for himself.

A breach has been made with the past, which allows us to envisage a new aspect of architecture corresponding to the technical civilization of the age we live in; the morphology of dead styles has been destroyed; and we are returning to honesty of thought and feeling. The general public, formerly profoundly indifferent to

Plate 1. The Fagus Boot-Last Factory at Alfeld-an-der-Leine, 1911 (in collaboration with Adolf Meyer).

everything to do with building, has been shaken out of its torpor; personal interest in architecture as something that concerns every one of us in our daily lives has been very widely aroused; and the broad lines of its future development are already clearly discernible. It is now becoming widely recognized that although the outward forms of the New Architecture differ fundamentally in an organic sense from those of the old, they are not the personal whims of a handful of architects avid for innovation at all cost, but simply the inevitable logical product of the intellectual, social and technical conditions of our age. A quarter of a century's earnest and pregnant struggle preceded their eventual emergence.

But the development of the New Architecture encountered serious obstacles at a very early stage of its development. Conflicting theories and the dogmas enunciated in architects' personal manifestos all helped to confuse the main issue. Technical difficulties were accentuated by the general economic decline that followed the war. Worst of all, 'modern' architecture became fashionable in several countries; with the result that formalistic imitation and snobbery

distorted the fundamental truth and simplicity on which this renascence was based.

That is why the movement must be purged from within if its original aims are to be saved from the strait-jacket of materialism and false slogans inspired by plagiarism or misconception. Catch phrases like 'functionalism' (*die neue Sachlichkeit*) and 'fitness for purpose = beauty' have had the effect of deflecting appreciation of the New Architecture into external channels or making it purely one-sided. This is reflected in a very general ignorance of the true motives of its founders: an ignorance that impels superficial minds, who do not perceive that the New Architecture is a bridge uniting opposite poles of thought, to relegate it to a single circumscribed province of design.

For instance rationalization, which many people imagine to be its cardinal principle, is really only its purifying agency. The liberation of architecture from a welter of ornament, the

---

Plate 2. The Entrance Front of the Administrative Office-Building in the Werkbund Exhibition at Cologne in 1914 (in collaboration with Adolf Meyer).

23

emphasis on its structural functions, and the concentration on concise and economical solutions, represent the purely material side of that formalizing process on which the *practical* value of the New Architecture depends. The other, the aesthetic satisfaction of the human soul, is just as important as the material. Both find their counterpart in that unity which is life itself. What is far more important than this structural economy and its functional emphasis is the intellectual achievement which has made possible a new spatial vision. For whereas building is merely a matter of methods and materials, architecture implies the mastery of space.

For the last century the transition from manual to machine production has so preoccupied humanity that, instead of pressing forward to tackle the new problems of design postulated by this unprecedented transformation, we have remained content to borrow our styles from antiquity and perpetuate historical prototypes in decoration.

That state of affairs is over at last. A new conception of building, based on realities, has emerged; and with it has come a new conception of space. These changes, and the superior technical resources we can now command as a direct result of them, are embodied in the very different appearance of the already numerous examples of the New Architecture.

Just think of all that modern technique has contributed to this decisive phase in the renascence of architecture, and the rapidity of its development!

Our fresh technical resources have furthered the disintegration of solid masses of masonry into slender piers, with consequent far-reaching economies in bulk, space, weight, and haulage. New synthetic substances—steel, concrete, glass—are actively superseding the traditional raw materials of construction. Their rigidity and molecular density have made it possible to erect wide-spanned and all but transparent structures for which the skill of previous ages was manifestly inadeqate. This enormous saving in structural volume was an architectural revolution in itself.

One of the outstanding achievements of the new constructional technique has been the abolition of the separating function of the wall. Instead of making the walls the element of support, as in a brick-built house, our new space-saving construction transfers the whole load of the structure to a steel or concrete framework. Thus the role of the walls becomes restricted to that of mere screens stretched between the upright columns of this framework to keep out rain, cold, and noise. In order to save weight and bulk still further, these non-supporting and now merely partitioning walls are made of light-weight pumice-concrete, breeze, or other reliable synthetic materials, in the form of hollow blocks or thin slabs. Systematic technical improvement in steel and concrete, and nicer and nicer calculation of their tensile and compressive strength, are steadily reducing the area occupied by supporting members. This, in turn, naturally leads to a progressively bolder (*i.e.* wider) opening up of the wall surfaces, which allows rooms to be much better lit. It is, therefore, only logical that the old type of window—a hole that had to be hollowed out of the full thickness of a support-

Plate 3. Rear View of the Administrative Office Building in the Werkbund Exhibition at Cologne in 1914 (in collaboration with Adolf Meyer).

ing wall—should be giving place more and more to the continuous horizontal casement, subdivided by thin steel mullions, characteristic of the New Architecture. And as a direct result of the growing preponderance of voids over solids, glass is assuming an ever greater structural importance. Its sparkling insubstantiality, and the way it seems to float between wall and wall imponderably as the air, adds a note of gaiety to our modern homes.

In the same way the flat roof is superseding the old penthouse roof with its tiled or slated gables. For its advantages are obvious: (1) light normally shaped top-floor rooms instead of poky attics, darkened by dormers and sloping ceilings, with their almost unutilizable corners; (2) the avoidance of timber rafters, so often the cause of fires; (3) the possibility of turning the top of the house to practical account as a sun loggia, open-air gymnasium, or children's playground; (4) simpler structural provision for subsequent additions, whether as extra stories or new wings; (5) elimination of unnecessary surfaces presented to the action of wind and weather, and therefore less need for repairs; (6) suppression of hanging gutters, external rain-pipes, etc., that often erode rapidly. With the development of air transport the architect will have to pay as much attention to the bird's-eye perspective of his houses as to their elevations. The utilization of flat roofs as 'grounds' offers us a means of re-acclimatizing nature amidst the stony deserts of our great towns; for the plots from which she has been evicted to make room for buildings can be given back to her up aloft. Seen from the skies, the leafy house-tops of the cities of the future will look like endless chains of hanging gardens. But the primary advantage of the flat roof is that it renders possible a much freer kind of interior planning.

Standardization

The elementary impulse of all national economy proceeds from the desire to meet the needs of the community at less cost and effort by the

Plate 4. The Municipal Theatre at Jena (reconstruction), 1922 (in collaboration with Adolf Meyer).

improvement of its productive organizations. This has led progressively to mechanization, specialized division of labour, and rationalization: seemingly irrevocable steps in industrial evolution which have the same implications for building as for every other branch of organized production. Were mechanization an end in itself it would be an unmitigated calamity, robbing life of half its fulness and variety by stunting men and women into sub-human, robot-like automatons. (Here we touch the deeper causality of the dogged resistance of the old civilization of handicrafts to the new world-order of the machine.) But in the last resort mechanization can have only one object: to abolish the individual's physical toil of providing himself with the necessities of existence in order that hand and brain may be set free for some higher order of activity.

Our age has initiated a rationalization of industry based on the kind of working partnership between manual and mechanical production we call standardization which is already having direct repercussions on building. There can be no doubt that the systematic application of standardization to housing would effect enor-

c   35

mous economies—so enormous, indeed, that it is impossible to estimate their extent at present.

Standardization is not an impediment to the development of civilization, but, on the contrary, one of its immediate prerequisites. A standard may be defined as that simplified practical exemplar of anything in general use which embodies a fusion of the best of its anterior forms —a fusion preceded by the elimination of the personal content of their designers and all otherwise ungeneric or non-essential features. Such an impersonal standard is called a 'norm' a word derived from a carpenter's square.

The fear that individuality will be crushed out by the growing 'tyranny' of standardization

Plate 5. Typical Products of the Bauhaus which were adopted as Models for Mass-Production by German Manufacturers, and also influenced Foreign Industrial Design (1922-1925). *a.* Models of Metal Lamps. *b.* Writing-Table in Glass, Metal and Wood. *c.* China Service designed by O. Lindig. *d.* Kitchen Equipment designed for the Haus am Horn at Weimar. *e.* Textiles designed by Otti Berger. *f.* First Models for Tubular Steel Furniture designed by Marcel Breuer.

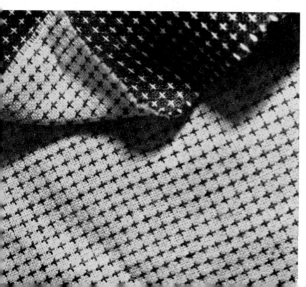

is the sort of myth which cannot sustain the briefest examination. In all great epochs of history the existence of standards—that is the conscious adoption of type-forms—has been the criterion of a polite and well-ordered society; for it is a commonplace that repetition of the same things for the same purposes exercises a settling and civilizing influence on men's minds.

As the basic cellular unit of that larger unit the street, the dwelling-house represents a typical group-organism. The uniformity of the cells whose multiplication by streets forms the still larger unit of the city therefore calls for formal expression. Diversity in their sizes provides the necessary modicum of variation, which in turn promotes natural competition between dissimilar types developing side by side. The most admired cities of the past are conclusive proof that the reiteration of 'typical' (*i.e.* typified) buildings notably enhances civic dignity and coherence. As a maturer and more final model than any of the individual prototypes merged in it, an accepted standard is always a formal common denominator of a whole period. The unification of architectural components would have the salutary effect of imparting that homogeneous character to our towns which is the distinguishing mark of a superior urban culture. A prudent limitation of variety to a few standard types of buildings increases their quality and decreases their cost; thereby raising the social level of the population as a whole. Proper respect for tradition will find a truer echo in these than in the miscellaneous solutions of an often arbitrary and aloof individualism because the greater communal utility of the former embodies a deeper architectural significance. The concentration of essential qualities in standard types presupposes methods of unprecedented industrial potentiality, which entail capital outlay on a scale that can only be justified by mass-production.

Rationalization

Building, hitherto an essentially manual trade, is already in course of transformation into an organized industry. More and more work that used to be done on the scaffolding is now carried out under factory conditions far away from the site. The dislocation which the seasonal character of building operations causes employers and employed alike—as, indeed, the community at large—is being gradually overcome. Continuous activity throughout the year will soon become the rule instead of the exception.

And just as fabricated materials have been evolved which are superior to natural ones in accuracy and uniformity, so modern practice in house construction is increasingly approximating to the successive stages of a manufacturing process. We are approaching a state of technical proficiency when it will become possible to rationalize buildings and mass-produce them in factories by resolving their structure into a number of component parts. Like boxes of toy bricks, these will be assembled in various formal compositions in a dry state: which means that building will definitely cease to be dependent on the weather. Ready-made houses of solid fireproof construction, that can be delivered fully equipped from stock, will ultimately become one of the principal products of industry. Before this is practicable, however, every part of the house—floor-beams, wall-slabs, windows, doors, staircases, and fittings—will have to be normed.

The repetition of standardized parts, and the use of identical materials in different buildings, will have the same sort of coordinating and sobering effect on the aspect of our towns as uniformity of type in modern attire has in social life. But that will in no sense restrict the architect's freedom of design. For although every house and block of flats will bear the unmistakable impress of our age, there will always remain, as in the clothes we wear, sufficient scope for the individual to find expression for his own personality. The net result should be a happy architectonic combination of maximum standardization and maximum variety. Since 1910 I have consistently advocated pre-fabrication of houses in numerous articles and lectures; besides which I have undertaken a number of practical experiments in this field of research in conjunction with important industrial concerns.

Dry assembly offers the best prospects because (to take only one of its advantages) moisture in one form or another is the principal obstacle to economy in masonry or brick construction (mortar joints). Moisture is the direct cause of most of the weaknesses of the old methods of building. It leads to badly fitting

joints, warping and staining, unforeseen piece-work, and serious loss of time and money through delays in drying. By eliminating this factor, and so assuring the perfect interlocking of all component parts, the pre-fabricated house makes it possible to guarantee a fixed price and a definite period of construction. Moreover the use of reliable modern materials enables the stability and insulation of a building to be increased and its weight and bulk decreased. A pre-fabricated house can be loaded on to a couple of lorries at the factory—walls, floors, roof, fittings and all—conveyed to the site, and put together in next to no time regardless of the season of the year.

The outstanding concomitant advantages of rationalized construction are superior economy and an enhanced standard of living. Many of the things that are regarded as luxuries today will be standard fitments in the homes of tomorrow.

So much for technique!—But what about beauty?

The New Architecture throws open its walls like curtains to admit a plenitude of fresh air,

Plate 6. The Bauhaus, Dessau, 1925.

43

daylight and sunshine. Instead of anchoring buildings ponderously into the ground with massive foundations, it poises them lightly, yet firmly, upon the face of the earth; and bodies itself forth, not in stylistic imitation or ornamental frippery, but in those simple and sharply modelled designs in which every part merges naturally into the comprehensive volume of the whole. Thus its aesthetic meets our material and psychological requirements alike.

For unless we choose to regard the satisfaction of those conditions which can alone animate, and so humanize, a room—spatial harmony, repose, proportion—as an ideal of some higher order, architecture cannot be limited to the fulfilment of its structural function.

We have had enough and to spare of the arbitrary reproduction of historic styles. In the progress of our advance from the vagaries of mere architectural caprice to the dictates of structural logic, we have learned to seek concrete expression of the life of our epoch in clear and crisply simplified forms.

Plate 7. The Bauhaus: A Corner of the Workshops' Wing.

Having briefly surveyed what the New Architecture has already achieved, and outlined the probable course of its development in the near future, I will turn back to my own part in its genesis. In 1908, when I finished my preliminary training and embarked on my career as an architect with Peter Behrens, the prevalent conceptions of architecture and architectural education were still entirely dominated by the academic stylisticism of the classical 'Orders'. It was Behrens who first introduced me to logical and systematical coordination in the handling of architectural problems. In the course of my active association with the important schemes on which he was then engaged, and frequent discussions with him and other prominent members of the *Deutscher Werkbund*, my own ideas began to crystallize as to what the essential nature of building ought to be. I became obsessed by the conviction that modern constructional technique could not be denied expression in architecture, and that that expression demanded the use of unprecedented forms. Dynamic as was the stimulus of Behrens's masterly teaching, I could not contain my growing impatience to start on my own account. In 1910 I set up in

47

independent practice. Shortly afterwards I was commissioned to design the *Faguswerke* at Alfeld-an-der-Leine (*Plate 1*) in conjunction with the late Adolf Meyer. This factory, and the buildings entrusted to me for the Cologne *Werk-bund* Exhibition of 1914 (*Plates 2* and *3*), clearly manifested the essential characteristics of my later work.

The full consciousness of my responsibility in advancing ideas based on my own reflections only came home to me as a result of the war, in which these theoretical premises first took definite shape. After that violent interruption, which kept me, like most of my fellow-architects, from work for four years, every thinking man felt the necessity for an intellectual change of front. Each in his own particular sphere of activity aspired to help in bridging the disastrous gulf between reality and idealism. It was then that the immensity of the mission of the architects of my own generation first dawned on me. I saw that an architect cannot hope to realize his ideas unless he can influence the in-

---

Plate 8. The Bauhaus: The Pupils' Hostel and Atelier Building.

dustry of his country sufficiently for a new school
of design to arise as a result; and unless that
school succeeds in acquiring authoritative significance. I saw, too, that to make this possible
would require a whole staff of collaborators and
assistants: men who would work, not automatically as an orchestra obeys its conductor's baton,
but independently, although in close cooperation, to further a common cause.

The Bauhaus

This idea of the fundamental unity underlying all branches of design was my guiding inspiration in founding the original *Bauhaus*.
During the war I had been summoned to an
audience with the Grand Duke of Sachsen-Wei-
mar-Eisenach to discuss my taking over the Weimar School of Arts and Crafts (*Grossherzogliche
Kunstgewerbeschule*) from the distinguished
Belgian architect, Henri Van de Velde, who had
himself suggested that I should be his successor.
Having asked for, and been accorded, full powers
in regard to reorganization I assumed control
of the Weimar School of Arts and Crafts, and

also of the Weimar Academy of Fine Art (*Gross-herzogliche Hochschule für Bildende Kunst*), in the spring of 1919. As a first step towards the realization of a much wider plan—in which my primary aim was that the principle of training the individual's natural capacities to grasp life as a whole, a single cosmic entity, should form the basis of instruction throughout the school instead of in only one or two arbitrarily 'special-ized' classes—I amalgamated these institutions into a *Hochschule für Gestaltung*, or High School for Design, under the name of *Das Staatliche Bauhaus Weimar*.

In carrying out this scheme I tried to solve the ticklish problem of combining imaginative design and technical proficiency. That meant finding a new and hitherto non-existent type of collaborator who could be moulded into being equally proficient in both. As a safeguard against any recrudescence of the old dilettante handi-craft spirit I made every pupil (including the architectural students) bind himself to complete his full legal term of apprenticeship in a formal letter of engagement registered with the local trades council. I insisted on manual instruction, not as an end in itself, or with any idea of turning it to incidental account by actually producing handicrafts, but as providing a good all-round training for hand and eye, and being a practical first step in mastering industrial processes.

The *Bauhaus* workshops were really laboratories for working out practical new designs for present-day articles and improving models for mass-production. To create type-forms that would meet all technical, aesthetic and commercial demands required a picked staff. It needed a body of men of wide general culture as thoroughly versed in the practical and mechanical sides of design as in its theoretical and formal laws. Although most parts of these prototype models had naturally to be made by hand, their constructors were bound to be intimately acquainted with factory methods of production and assembly, which differ radically from the practices of handicraft. It is to its intrinsic particularity that each different type of machine owes the 'genuine stamp' and 'individual beauty' of its products. Senseless imitation of hand-made goods by machinery infallibly bears the mark of a makeshift substitute. The *Bauhaus* represented a school of thought which believes that the difference between industry and handicraft is due, far less to the different nature of the tools employed in each, than to subdivision of labour in the one and undivided control by a single workman in the other. Handicrafts and industry may be regarded as opposite poles that are gradually approaching each other. The former have already begun to change their traditional nature. In the future the field of handicrafts will be found to lie mainly in the preparatory stages of evolving experimental new type-forms for mass-production.

There will, of course, always be talented craftsmen who can turn out individual designs and find a market for them. The *Bauhaus*, however, deliberately concentrated primarily on what has now become a work of paramount urgency: to avert mankind's enslavement by the machine by giving its products a content of reality and significance, and so saving the home from mechanistic anarchy. This meant evolving goods specifically designed for mass-production. Our object was to eliminate every drawback of the machine without sacrificing any one of its real advantages. We aimed at realizing standards of excellence, not creating transient novelties.

When the *Bauhaus* was four years old, and all the essentials of its organization had been definitely established, it could already look back on initial achievements that had commanded widespread attention in Germany and abroad. It was then that I decided to set forth my views. These had naturally developed considerably in the light of experience, but they had not undergone any substantial change as a result. The pages which follow are abstracted from this essay, which was published in 1923 under the title of *Idee und Aufbau des Staatlichen Bauhauses* (The Conception and Realization of the Bauhaus).

The art of building is contingent on the co-ordinated team-work of a band of active collaborators whose orchestral cooperation symbolizes the cooperative organism we call society. Architecture and design in a general sense are consequently matters of paramount concern to the nation at large. There is a widespread heresy that art is just a useless luxury. This is

Plate 9. Professor Gropius's own House at Dessau, 1925.

one of our fatal legacies from a generation which arbitrarily elevated some of its branches above the rest as the 'Fine Arts', and in so doing robbed all of their basic identity and common life. The typical embodiment of the *l'art pour l'art* mentality, and its chosen instrument, was 'the Academy'. By depriving handicrafts and industry of the informing services of the artist the academies drained them of their vitality, and brought about the artist's complete isolation from the community. Art is not one of those things that may be imparted. Whether a design be the outcome of knack or creative impulse depends on individual propensity. But if what we call art cannot be taught or learnt, a thorough knowledge of its principles and of sureness of hand can be. Both are as necessary for the artist of genius as for the ordinary artisan.

What actually happened was that the academies turned out an 'artistic proletariat' foredoomed to semi-starvation. Lulled by false hopes of the rewards of genius, this soon numerous class was brought up to the 'professions' of architect, painter, sculptor, etc., without the requisite training to give it an independent artistic volition and to enable it to find its feet in the

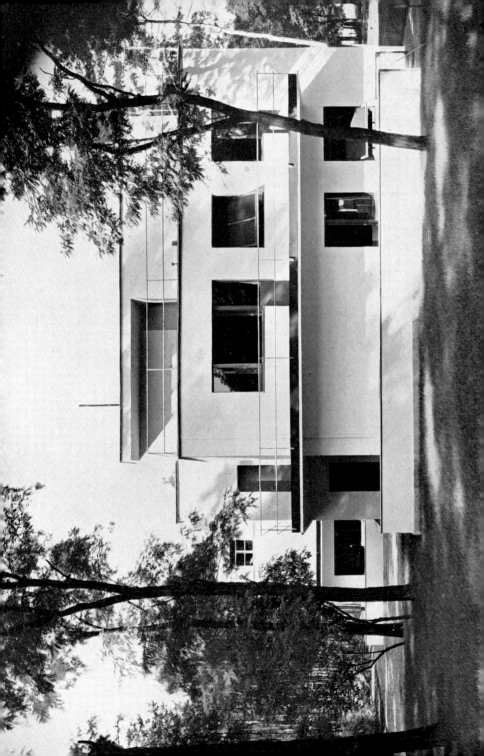

struggle for existence. Thus such skill as it acquired was of that amateurish studio-bred order which is innocent of realities like technical progress and commercial demand. The besetting vice of the academy schools was that they were obsessed by that rare 'biological' sport', the commanding genius; and forgot that their business was to teach drawing and painting to hundreds and hundreds of minor talents, barely one in a thousand of whom could be expected to have the makings of a real architect or painter. In the vast majority of cases this hopelessly one-sided instruction condemned its pupils to the lifelong practice of a purely sterile art. Had these hapless drones been given a proper practical training they could have become useful members of society.

The rise of the academies spelt the gradual decay of the spontaneous traditional art that had permeated the life of the whole people. All that remained was a 'Salon Art', entirely remote from everyday life, which by the middle of the XIXth Century had petered out into mere exercises in individual virtuosity. It was

Plate 10. A Pair of Semi-Detached Houses for the Staff of the Bauhaus, 1925.

then that a revolt began. Ruskin and Morris strove to find a means of reuniting the world of art with the world of work. Towards the end of the century their lead was followed by Van de Velde, Olbrich, Behrens and others on the Continent. This movement, which started with the building of the 'Artists' Colony' at Darmstadt and culminated in the founding of the *Deutscher Werkbund* in Munich, led to the establishment of *Kunstgewerbeschulen* in the principal German towns. These were intended to give the rising generation of artists a practical training for handicrafts and industry. But the academic spirit was too firmly implanted for that 'practical training' to be more than a dilettante smattering. The *projet* and the 'composition' still held pride of place in their curricula. The first attempts to get away from the old unreal art-for-art's-sake attitude failed because they were not planned on a sufficiently wide front and did not go deep enough to touch the root of the evil.

Notwithstanding, commerce, and more particularly industry, began to look towards the artist. There was a genuine ambition to supplement efficiency by beauty of shape and finish: things which the working technician was not in

a position to supply. So manufacturers bought 'artistic designs'. But these paper aids proved broken reeds. The artist was a man 'remote from the world', at once too unpractical and too unfamiliar with technical requirements to be able to assimilate his conceptions of form to the processes of manufacture. On the other hand the business man and the technician lacked sufficient foresight to realize that the combination of form, efficiency and economy they desired could only be obtained by recognizing painstaking cooperation with a responsible artist as part of the routine of production. Since the kind of designer to fill this gap was non-existent, the future training of artistic talent clearly demanded a thorough practical grounding under factory conditions combined with sound theoretical instruction in the laws of design.

Thus the *Bauhaus* was inaugurated with the specific object of realizing a modern architectonic art, which, like human nature, should be all-embracing in its scope. Within that sovereign federative union all the different 'arts' (with the

---

Plate 11. A Block of Two-and-a-Half-Roomed Flats in the Siemensstadt *Siedlung*, Berlin, 1929.

various manifestations and tendencies of each)
—every branch of design, every form of technique—could be coordinated and find their
appointed place. Our ultimate goal, therefore,
was the composite but inseparable work of art,
the great building, in which the old dividing-
line between monumental and decorative elements would have disappeared for ever.

The quality of a man's creative work depends
on a proper balance of his faculties. It is not
enough to train one or other of these, since all
alike need to be developed. That is why manual
and mental instruction in design were given
simultaneously.

The actual curriculum consisted of:

(1) *Practical Instruction* in the handling of
Stone, Wood, Metal, Clay, Glass, Pigments,
Textile-Looms; supplemented by lessons in the
use of Materials and Tools, and a grounding in
Book-Keeping, Costing and the Drawing-Up of
Tenders: and

(2) *Formal Instruction* under the following
heads:

(*a*) *Aspect*
      The Study of Nature
      The Study of Materials

(*b*) *Representation*

The Study of Plane Geometry

The Study of Construction

Draughtsmanship

Model-Making

(*c*) *Design*

The Study of Volumes

The Study of Colours

The Study of Composition

supplemented by lectures on all branches of art (both ancient and modern) and science (including elementary biology and sociology).

The full course covered three periods:

(1) *Preparatory Instruction*, lasting six months, which consisted of elementary training in design and experiments with different materials in the special Beginners' Workshop.

(2) *Technical Instruction* (supplemented by more advanced instruction in design) as a legally bound apprentice in one of the Training Workshops. This lasted three years, at the end of which the pupil (if proficient enough) obtained his Journeyman's Certificate either from the local trades council or the *Bauhaus* itself.

(3) *Structural Instruction* for especially promising pupils, the duration of which varied

according to the circumstances and talents of the individual concerned. This consisted of an alternation between manual work on actual building sites and theoretic training in the Research Department of the *Bauhaus*, which amplified the Practical and Formal Instruction he had already received. At the end of his Structural Instruction the pupil (if proficient enough) obtained his Master-Builder's Diploma either from the local trades council or the *Bauhaus* itself.

Preparatory Instruction

Applicants were selected on the basis of their probable aptitudes, which were judged by the specimens of their work they were required to submit. This method of selection was obviously liable to error since there is no known anthropometric system to gauge a man's continually changing powers of development.

The pupil started with the six-months preparatory course, which embraced the whole range of the *Bauhaus* teaching in an elementary

Plate 12. A Block of Three-and-a-Half-Roomed Flats in the Siemensstadt *Siedlung*, Berlin, 1929.

form. Practical and formal subjects were taught side by side so as to develop the pupil's creative powers and enable him to grasp the physical nature of materials and the basic laws of design. Instruction was confined to observation and representation (with the object of inculcating the ideal identity of form and content); associations with any kind of 'style' were studiously avoided.[1] The first task was to liberate the pupil's individuality from the dead weight of conventions and allow him to acquire that personal experience and self-taught knowledge which are the only means of realizing the natural limitations of our creative powers. That is why collective work was not considered important at this stage. Subjective and objective observation, and the laws of representational and abstract design, were taught turn and turn about. Even ordinary pedagogic education can be made to act as a powerful stimulus in these respects.

The Preparatory Instruction was intended to help us to arrive at a just appreciation of the

[1] This course was based on the method of teaching first introduced by Johannes Itten in Vienna in 1918, and subsequently developed by him in the *Bauhaus* itself. Our Preparatory Instruction was still further developed by Professor Moholy-Nagy and Professor Josef Albers (*vide* Professor Moholy-Nagy's *Von Material zu Architektur* published by Albert Langen, Munich).

71

pupil's powers of expression, which obviously varied considerably. All the work done during this period was naturally influenced by his teachers. It possessed importance only in so far as elementary self-expression that has been systematically developed is the foundation of all art which deserves the epithet 'creative'. Whether a pupil was then allowed to enter one or other of the Training Workshops depended on his personal capacity and the quality evinced by his work.

Practical and Formal Instruction

The best kind of practical teaching is the old system of free apprenticeship to a master-craftsman, which was devoid of any scholastic taint. Those old master-craftsmen possessed practical and formal skill in equal measure. But as they no longer exist it is impossible to revive voluntary apprenticeship. All we can substitute for it is a synthetic method of bringing practical and formal influences to bear on the pupil simultaneously by combining the teaching of first-

Plate 13. The *Siedlung* of Working-Class Dwellings at Dessau, with their Co-operative Stores in the foreground, 1928.

rate technicians with that of artists of outstanding merit. A dual education of this kind would enable the coming generation to achieve the reunion of all forms of creative work and become the architects of a new civilization. That was why we made it a rule in the *Bauhaus* that every pupil and apprentice had to be taught throughout by two masters working in the closest collaboration with each other; and that no pupil or apprentice could be excused from attending the classes of either. The Practical Instruction was the most important part of our preparation for collective work, and also the most effective way of combating arty-crafty tendencies.

Believing the machine to be our modern medium of design we sought to come to terms with it. But it would have been madness to turn over gifted pupils to the tender mercies of industry without any training in craftsmanship in the fond hope of thereby restoring 'the lost chord' between the artist and the world of work. Such idealism could only have resulted in their being overwhelmed by the narrow materialism and one-sided outlook of the modern factory. Since craftsmanship concentrates the whole sequence of manufacture in one and the same man's hands it would provide a nearer approximation to their intellectual status, and therefore offer them a better kind of practical training. Yet division of labour can no more be abandoned than the machine itself. If the spread of machinery has, in fact, destroyed the old basic unity of a nation's production the cause lies neither in the machine nor in its logical consequence of functionally differentiated processes of fabrication, but in the predominantly materialistic mentality of our age and the defective and unreal articulation of the individual to the community. The *Bauhaus* was anything but a school of arts and crafts, if only because a deliberate return to something of that kind would have meant simply putting back the clock. For now, as ever, man goes on improving his tools in order to spare himself more and more physical toil and increase his leisure proportionately.

The Practical Instruction was intended to prepare the pupil for work on standardization. Starting with the simplest tools and methods he gradually acquired the necessary understanding and skill for more complicated ones, which culminated in the application of machinery. But at no stage was he allowed to lose the formative thread of an organic process of production as the factory-worker inevitably does. Intimate contact between the various *Bauhaus* workshops and those of industrial concerns were deliberately cultivated as being of mutual advantage.[1] In the latter he obtained a superior degree of technical knowledge, and also learned the hard lesson that commercial insistence on the fullest utilization of time and plant was something which has to be taken directly into account by the modern designer. That respect for stern realities which is one of the strongest bonds between workers engaged on a common task speedily dissipated the misty aestheticism of the academies.

After three years' practical training the apprentice had to execute a design of his own

[1] By agreement with certain manufacturing firms, our ripest and most promising apprentices were sent to work for short periods in factories whose products corresponded with the particular branches of industrial design taught in the workshops they happened to be attached to at the *Bauhaus*. There they studied current industrial methods of production, manufacturing processes, price calculations, and possibilities for improving existing models and introducing new ones. The special knowledge they acquired in this way enabled them to be assigned to our Research Station on their return. In it they worked out new models under their former masters to meet the particular technical requirements of the firms they had been sent to. They further assisted these firms by keeping in close contact with the preparations for adjusting their machinery to produce them.

before, and to the satisfaction of, a panel of master-craftsmen for his Journeyman's Certificate. Any pupil in possession of this certificate could present himself for the Bauhaus Apprenticeship Examination, which demanded a much higher standard of proficiency (particularly in regard to individual aptitude for design) than the Journeyman's Certificate of Craftsmanship.

Thus our pupils' intellectual education proceeded hand in hand with their practical training. Instead of receiving arbitrary and subjective ideas of design they had objective tuition in the basic laws of form and colour, and the primary condition of the elements of each, which enabled them to acquire the necessary mental equipment to give tangible shape to their own creative instincts. Only those who have been taught how to grasp the comprehensive coherence of a larger design, and incorporate original work of their own as an integral part of it, are ripe for active cooperation in building. What is called 'the freedom of the artist' does not imply the unlimited command of a wide variety of different techniques and media, but simply his ability to design freely within the pre-ordained limits imposed by any one of them. Even today a knowledge of counterpoint is essential for a musical composer. That is now the solitary example of the theoretic basis every one of the arts formerly possessed but all the others have lost: something, in fact, which the designer must rediscover for himself. But though theory is in no sense a ready-made formula for a work of art it certainly remains the most important prerequisite of collective design. For since theory represents the impersonal cumulative experience of successive generations it offers a solid foundation on which a resolute band of fellow-workers can rear a higher embodiment of creative unity than the individual artist. Accordingly the *Bauhaus* had to assist in preparing the ground for an eventual reorganization of the whole field of design along these lines—without which its ultimate goal would needs remain unattainable.

The sort of collaboration we aimed at was not simply a matter of pooling knowledge and talents. A building designed by one man and carried out for him by a number of purely executant associates cannot hope to achieve more than superficial unity. Our ideal was that what each collaborator contributed to the common task should be something he had devised as well as wrought himself. In cooperation of this kind formal unity must be maintained, and this can only be done by a recurrent reiteration of the proportions of the *motif* dominating the whole in each of its component parts. Every collaborator therefore needs to have a clear realization of the comprehensive master design, and the reasons for its adoption.

Structural Instruction

As has already been indicated, only fully qualified apprentices were considered sufficiently mature for active collaboration in building; and only the pick of them were admitted to our Research Station and the Designing Studio attached to it. These chosen few were also given access to all the different workshops so as to gain insight into branches of technique other than their own. Their practical training for cooperative work was always on the scaffolding of an actual building-site, but its nature varied according to the opportunities afforded by the outside contracts which the *Bauhaus* happened to have on hand at the moment. This enabled them to learn the correlation of everything that comes within the scope of building practice while earning their keep. In so far as our curriculum did not provide finishing courses in the theoretical side of the more specialized branches of engineering—such as steel and concrete construction, heating, plumbing, etc.—or advanced statics, mechanics and physics, it was usually found advisable to let the most promising of the architectural pupils round off their studies by attending complementary classes at various technical institutes. As a matter of principle every apprentice on completing his training was encouraged to go and work for a time in a factory to familiarize himself with industrial machinery and acquire business experience.

The prime essential for fruitful collaboration on the part of our pupils was a complete understanding of the aims that have inspired the New Architecture.

During the course of the last two or three generations architecture degenerated into a florid aestheticism, as weak as it was sentimental, in which the art of building became synonymous with meticulous concealment of the verities of structure under a welter of heterogeneous ornament. Bemused with academic conventions, architects lost touch with the rapid progress of technical developments and let the planning of our towns escape them. Their 'architecture' was that which the *Bauhaus* emphatically rejected. A modern building should derive its architectural significance solely from the vigour and consequence of its own organic proportions. It must be true to itself, logically transparent and virginal of lies or trivialities, as befits a direct affirmation of our contemporary world of mechanization and rapid transit. The increasingly daring lightness of modern constructional methods has banished the crushing sense of ponderosity inseparable from the solid walls and massive foundations of masonry. And with its disappearance the old obsession for the hollow sham of axial symmetry is giving place to the vital rhythmic equilibrium of free asymmetrical grouping.

The direct affinity between the tight economy of space and material in industry and structures based on these principles is bound to condition the future planning of our towns. It is therefore the primary duty of everyone who aspires to be a builder to grasp the significance

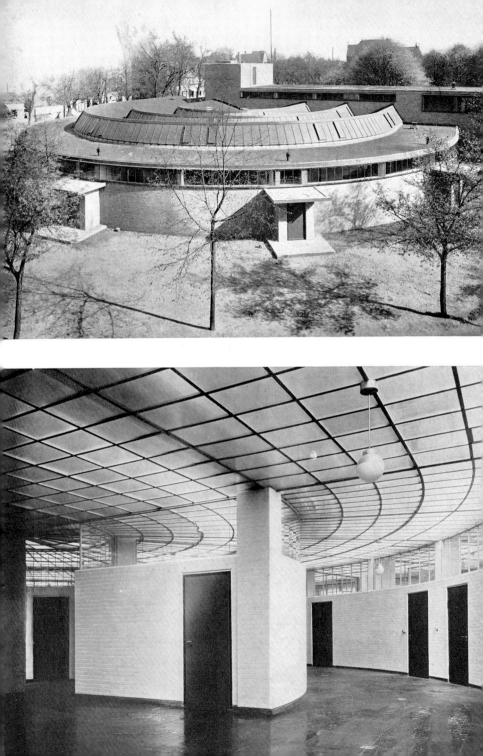

of the New Architecture and realize the factors which have determined its characteristics: a manifold simplicity arrived at by deliberate restriction to certain basic forms used repetitively; and the structural subdivision of buildings according to their nature, and that of the streets they face.

This was at once the limit of our Structural Instruction and the culminating point of the entire *Bauhaus* teaching. Any pupil who could prove he had thoroughly absorbed the whole of it and evinced adequate technical proficiency received his Master-Builder's Diploma.

What we preached in practice was the common citizenship of all forms of creative work, and their logical interdependence on one another in the modern world. We wanted to help the formal artist to recover the fine old sense of design and execution being one, and make him feel that the drawing-board is merely a prelude to the active joy of fashioning. Building unites

Plate 14. The Dessau Labour Exchange, 1929. (*Top*) Applicants' Entrance. (*Bottom*) Interior View.

both manual and mental workers in a common task. Therefore all alike, artist as artisan, should have a common training; and since experimental and productive work are of equal practical importance the basis of that training should be broad enough to give every kind of talent an equal chance. As varieties of talent cannot be distinguished before they manifest themselves, the individual must be able to discover his proper sphere of activity in the course of his own development. Naturally the great majority will be absorbed by the building trades, industry, etc. But there will always be a small minority of outstanding ability whose legitimate ambitions it would be folly to circumscribe. As soon as this *élite* has finished its communal training it will be free to concentrate on individual work, contemporary problems, or that inestimably useful speculative research to which humanity owes the sort of values stockbrokers call 'futures'. And since all these commanding brains will have been through the same industrial mill they will know, not only how to make industry adopt their improvements and inventions, but also how to make the machine the vehicle of their ideas. Men of this stamp are sure to be eagerly sought after.

The *Bauhaus* felt it had a double moral responsibility: to make its pupils fully conscious of the age they were living in; and to train them to turn their native intelligence, and the knowledge they received, to practical account in the design of type-forms which would be the direct expression of that consciousness.

As our struggle with prevailing ideas proceeded, the *Bauhaus* was able to clarify its own aims in the process of getting to grips with the problem of design from every angle and formulating its periodic discoveries. Our guiding principle was that artistic design is neither an intellectual nor a material affair, but simply an integral part of the stuff of life. Further, that the revolution in aesthetics has given us fresh insight into the meaning of design, just as the mechanization of industry has provided new tools for its realization. Our ambition was to rouse the creative artist from his other-world-

Plate 15. Copper-Plate Houses designed for Mass-Production, 1932: (*Top*) A Complete Five-Roomed House loaded on a Motor Lorry for Conveyance to the Site. (*Middle*) Dry Assembly of the Walls. (*Bottom*) The Completed House.

89

liness and reintegrate him into the workaday world of realities; and at the same time to broaden and humanize the rigid, almost exclusively material, mind of the business man. Thus our informing conception of the basic unity of all design in relation to life was in diametrical opposition to that of 'art for art's sake', and the even more dangerous philosophy it sprang from: business as an end in itself.

This explains our (by no means exclusive) concentration on the design of technical products, and the organic sequence of their processes of manufacture, which gave rise to an erroneous idea that the *Bauhaus* had set itself up as the apotheosis of rationalism. In reality, however, we were far more preoccupied with exploring the territory that is common to the formal and technical spheres, and defining where they cease to coincide. The standardization of the practical machinery of life implies no robotization of the individual, but, on the contrary, the unburdening of his existence from much unnecessary dead-weight so as to leave him freer to develop on a higher plane. Efficient and well-oiled machinery of daily life cannot of course constitute an end in itself, but it at least for ms a point of departure for the acquisition of a maximum of personal freedom and independence. An intellectual economy naturally takes longer to perfect than a material one, since it requires more knowledge and mental self-discipline. Here, at the focal point where civilization and culture meet, a clearer light is shed on the fundamental difference between an ordinary commercial product, the humble output of a calculating brain, and the work of art, the fruit of what William Blake called 'mental strife'. It is true that a work of art remains a technical product, but it has an intellectual purpose to fulfil as well which only passion and imagination can achieve.

The practical objectivity of the *Bauhaus* teaching explains why, in spite of the diversity of its collaborators, its productions were characterized by a basic uniformity. This was the result of the development of a common intellectual outlook to supersede the old aesthetic conception of form as understood by the Arts and Crafts Movement.

But we had also to hold our own in another direction: against detractors who sought to identify every building and object in which ornament seemed to be discarded as examples of an imaginary 'Bauhaus Style'; and imitators who prostituted our fundamental precepts into modish trivialities. The object of the *Bauhaus* was not to propagate any 'style', system, dogma, formula, or vogue, but simply to exert a revitalizing influence on design. We did not base our teaching on any preconceived ideas of form, but sought the vital spark of life behind life's ever-changing forms. The *Bauhaus* was the first institution in the world to dare to embody this principle in a definite curriculum. To further the cause of its ideals, and maintain the vigour and alertness of that community spirit in which imagination and reality can alone be fused, it had to assume the responsibilities of leadership. A 'Bauhaus Style' would have been a confession of failure and a return to that very stagnation and devitalizing inertia which I had called it into being to combat.

Plate 16. Project for a Group of Ten-Storey Blocks of Dwellings: (*Top*) With Wide Intervals between the Blocks. (*Bottom*) Planned for Erection along the Bank of a River or the Shore of a Lake.

In 1925 the *Bauhaus* migrated to Dessau: a move which coincided with an important change in its organization. The dual control of each workshop by a teacher of design and a practical instructor was now superseded by that of a single master. In point of fact the fusion of their separate spheres had (as was hoped) been automatically effected in the course of training the first generation. Five old *Bauhaus* students were now chosen as heads of the new workshops.[1]

In connection with the transference from

[1] Even after the *Bauhaus* had moved to Dessau it could only rely on a relatively very small income, which was defrayed by an annual vote from the municipality. Including the salaries of teachers, etc.—of whom there were about 24 to 180-200 pupils —the total grant amounted to some 100,000 Reichsmarks (then slightly under £5000). In addition to this, however, the town had to meet the interest and annual reduction charges on the capital outlay represented by the new buildings and their equipment, which had cost somewhere about 850,000 Reichsmarks (at that time roughly equivalent to £42,450). The royalties from the licences we granted to various firms for the mass-production of *Bauhaus* models (Furniture, Carpets, Textiles, China, Electric-Light Fittings, etc) contributed a subsidiary source of revenue which steadily increased as time went on.

My desire to keep fees very low, and to provide as many free places as possible for talented but impecunious pupils, had the official support of the municipal authorities. I was able also to pay pupils for any of their *Bauhaus* work that proved saleable: an arrangement which assured many of them a (necessarily very straitened) means of subsistence during their three-years course of training.

Weimar the town council of Dessau commissioned me to design a comprehensive group of buildings: a new and *ad hoc* Bauhaus (*Plates 6, 7* and *8*), a labour-exchange (*Plate 14*), and a housing colony (*Plate 13*). For their construction and equipment I brought the whole body of teachers and students into active cooperation. The acid test of attempting to coordinate several different branches of design in the actual course of building proved entirely successful; and this without the self-sufficiency of its component parts suffering any prejudice. On the contrary, the effect on the individual pupil of transforming the school into a site for building operations was to increase his moral stature by virtue of the direct responsibility that now rested on him. The band of fellow-workers inspired by a common will and purpose I once dreamed of had become a reality and an example that could not fail to make itself felt in the outside world. In the period which followed several art schools and technical colleges at home and abroad adopted the *Bauhaus* curriculum as their pattern. German industry began to mass-produce *Bauhaus* models and to seek our collaboration in the design of new ones. Many

96

former *Bauhaus* pupils obtained prominent positions in industrial concerns on account of their all-round training; others were appointed to teaching posts in foreign institutes. In short, the intellectual objective of the *Bauhaus* had been fully attained.

In 1928, when I felt that the stability and future of the *Bauhaus* were assured, I handed over control to my successor; and returned to practice in Berlin where I could devote more of my time to the sociological and structural aspects of housing.

As one of the vice-chairmen of the *Reichsforschungsgesellschaft für Wirtschaftlichkeit im Bau-und Wohnungswesen* (our National Society for Research into Economic Building and Housing) I was naturally brought into immediate contact with the practical side of those very problems which the *Bauhaus* had been planned to deal with. The *Reichsforschungsgesellschaft* was instrumental in promoting an important competition for the lay-out and development of a large tract of building land on the outskirts of Berlin. In that competition (in which the majority of German architects took part), as in another on a similar scale for rehousing at Karlsruhe, my designs were awarded the first prize; and the latter town appointed me as chief architect for the construction of what is known as the Dammerstock *Siedlung*. Other housing schemes were also entrusted to me, notably one in the industrial Siemensstadt district of Berlin (*Plates 11* and *12*). But in all this interesting work the questions that engrossed me most were the minimum dwelling for the lowest-paid section of the community; the middle-class home regarded as an economically equipped unit complete in itself; and what structural form each ought logically to assume—whether as part of a multi-storied block, a flat in a building of medium height, or a small separate house. And beyond these again loomed the rational form for the whole city as a planned organism.

My idea of the architect as a coordinator—whose business it is to unify the various formal, technical, social and economic problems that arise in connection with building—inevitably led me on step by step from study of the function of the house to that of the street; from the street to the town; and finally to the still vaster implications of regional and national planning.

I believe that the New Architecture is destined to dominate a far more comprehensive sphere than building means today; and that from the investigation of its details we shall advance towards an ever-wider and profounder conception of design as one great cognate whole —the mirror of the indivisibility and immensity and underlying unity of life itself, of which it is an integral part. It looks as though the mastery of the machine, the conquest of a new appreciation of space, and the pioneering work of finding the essential common denominator for the new forms of building had almost exhausted the creative powers of the architects of this generation. The next will accomplish that refinement of these forms which will lead to their generalization.

But I must return to Town-Planning, at once the most burning and baffling problem of all.

The rapid increase in our means of locomotion, and the consequent readjustment of the old coefficient of time as the factor of distance, has begun to break down the frontiers between town and country. Modern men and women require contrast both as recreation and stimulus. The nostalgia of the town-dweller for the country and the countryman's for the town are the expression of a deep-rooted and growing desire that clamours for satisfaction. Technical developments are transplanting urban civilization into the countryside and re-acclimatizing nature in the heart of the city. The demand for more spacious, and above all greener and sunnier, cities has now become insistent. Its corollary is the separation of residential from industrial and commercial districts by the provision of properly coordinated transport services. Thus the goal of the modern town-planner should be to bring town and country into closer and closer relationship.

Opinion is still very much divided as to the ideal form of dwelling for the bulk of the population: structurally separate houses with gardens of their own; tenement blocks of medium height (2-5 floors); or 8-12 storied buildings.

The decisive consideration for the townsman in the choice of a dwelling is utility. What that utility is depends on the nature of his profession, the extent of his income, and his personal tastes. To more people than not the separate house naturally seems the most welcome haven

100

of refuge in the wilderness of a great city. Its greater seclusion, the sense of complete possession, and the direct communication with a garden are assets which everyone can appreciate. All the same the tenement block is a true embodiment of the needs of our age, but we should not allow ourselves to be resigned to it in its present stage of development and regard it purely as a necessary evil. We must not allow its obvious defects to deter us from reconsidering its practical possibilities in a fresh light.

Tenements have fallen into ill repute because so few advantages can be claimed for existing examples of the 3-5 storied type. The intervals between the blocks are usually far too narrow, which results in the area of the surrounding gardens (if any) being as inadequate as the angle of isolation. When conscientiously planned 8-12 are substituted for 3-5 storied blocks these drawbacks disappear. Dwellings of this kind satisfy all requirements in regard to light, air, tranquillity and rapid egress; besides offering many conveniences it is almost impossible to provide in private houses. Instead of the ground-floor window looking on to blank walls, or into cramped and sunless courtyards, they command a clear view of the sky over the broad expanses of grass and trees which separate the blocks and serve as playgrounds for the children. Thus an oasis of verdure can be created in the midst of the stony desert of streets. And where the flat roofs of these tall buildings are laid out with gardens as well the last terror inspired by that unhappy name 'tenements' will have been banished for ever. As citizens of a green city the inhabitants will find that contact with Nature ceases to mean an occasional Sunday outing and becomes a daily experience.

The form of housing called *Flachbau* in German—structurally separate houses with gardens of their own—is anything but a sovereign specific, for if *Flachbau* were carried to its logical conclusion the result would be such a disintegration of the town as would spell its antithesis. Our aim should be a looser, not a more sprawling type of plan. Horizontal and vertical housing, *Flachbau* and *Hochbau*, ought to be developed side by side. We should restrict the former to outer suburban areas with a low building density, and the latter to the populous central areas (here the need for it has been conclusively established) in the form of 8-12 storied blocks

102

with all the usual communal conveniences. Blocks of intermediate height (*Mittelbau*) have the advantages neither of small houses nor of multi-storied flats. The abandonment of this type would therefore clearly be a step in the right direction.

The Third Conference of the International Congress of Modern Architecture passed a resolution that all countries should be urged to investigate the skyscraper tenement-block from the sociological and economic points of view because so few data were available as to its practical suitability.

By what means can we overcome the defects of our urban buildings—their lack of light and air, their noisiness, and their paucity of space? If the city is to be confined to the smallest superficial area in order that minimum distances from one business centre to another may be maintained, then there is only one rational solution for securing better light and air and—paradoxical as it may sound—an increase in living-space: the multiplication of floors. Let us assume it has been decided to erect free-standing blocks of flats on a north by south diagonal; and that the site measures approxi-

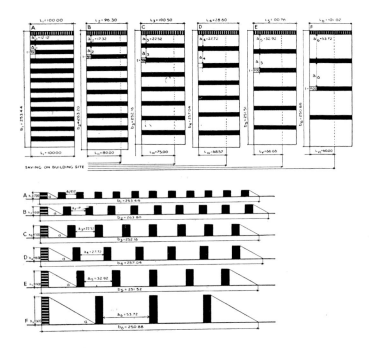

Diagrams illustrating the Development of a Rectangular Building-Site with Parallel Rows of Tenement-Blocks of Different Heights.

In the two comparative diagrams above, the interval between the blocks, though varying according to the number of their floors (2, 3, 4, 5, 6 and 10 respectively), has in every case been fixed so as to give the same (30 degrees) angle of light from the ground-line of one block to the roof-parapet of that standing next to it.

Result: With an identical angle of light the number of beds (reckoning 45 square feet of living-space to each bed—*i.e.* per inhabitant) increases with the number of floors; the 1200 beds of the ten three-storied blocks mounting to a total of 1700 in the four ten-storied ones

The two comparative diagrams on the opposite page illustrate how an identical amount of living-space (reckoning 160 square feet per head) can be provided on sites of equal area by blocks of different heights (2, 3, 4, 5, 6 and 10 floors respectively); the density of population therefore remaining the same.

104

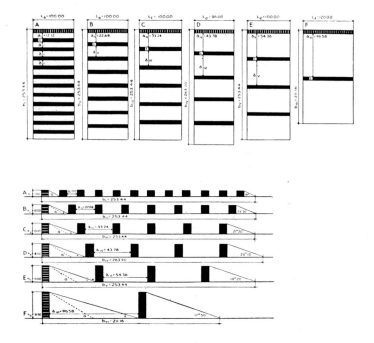

Result: In proportion as the number of floors increases the angle of light between the blocks decreases. Thus the higher blocks enjoy better isolation, and insure a more rational utilization of the size by providing a greater ratio of green open space per inhabitant. For instance, while the interval between the three-storied blocks is about double their height, it becomes almost triple in the case of the ten-storied ones; the corresponding ratio of planted grounds per inhabitant rising from approximately 135 square feet in the former to some 250 square feet in the latter.

Moral: Existing legislation limiting density of population is superannuated in so far as it restricts the maximum height of buildings. We need new laws restricting density of population in terms of the maximum amount of floor-space per acre of building land, but abolishing existing limitations on the height of buildings.

Ten to twelve storied tenement-blocks make the ideal of 'the City Verdant' a practical possibility.

105

mately 300 × 750 feet. Now if we compare the possibilities in regard to space utilization and light in the case of 2-3-5 storied buildings on the one hand, and 10-storied buildings on the other, the following surprising results are obtained:

1. Given an equal angle of light between the blocks (say 30 degrees) the amount of utilizable area *increases* with the number of stories. In comparison with two-storied, ten-storied blocks have over 60 per cent. more utilizable superficial area; and this in spite of the fact that they enjoy the same amount of light and air.

2. If we convert utilization into terms of economy in building land; that is to say if, assuming an equal angle of light for each of the blocks, we divide an identical extent of floor-space between them, we find there is a saving of about 40 per cent. with the ten-storied as against the two-storied ones—again in spite of each enjoying the same amount of light and air.

3. If, however, we estimate utilization purely in terms of light and air—that is to say if we neither reduce the amount of building land nor increase the utilizable superficial area—we find that the angle of light between the blocks falls

from 30 degrees in the case of the two-storied to 17·50 degrees in the case of the ten-storied blocks. In other words we gain the immense advantage of a much more generous amount of light, sun and air through having an almost ten times wider interval between the blocks than in the case of two-storied buildings—again without any corresponding practical drawbacks. Valuable space is made available for car-parking between the blocks, and shops can be built along their rear as well as their front elevations.

It is evident, therefore, that the height-limit imposed by regulations is an irrational restriction which has hampered evolution in design. Restriction of the number of dwellings per acre is, of course, a very necessary safeguard, but one that has nothing to do with the height of the buildings concerned. Overcrowding can be far more effectively combated by reducing their maximum floor area or total cubic volume. That is what we ought to press for in the first place! If the data just cited were systematically applied it would be possible to improve the lighting and ventilation of the business quarters, widen their streets wholesale (with a consequent abatement in noise); and yet substantially increase the amount of available floor-space. In the course of the recurrent controversies over the adoption of skyscraper construction in European cities the peculiarity of American conditions has become a sort of red herring for both sides. That the skyscraper districts of New York and Chicago are a planless chaos is no argument *per se* against the expediency of multi-storied office-buildings. The problem is one that can only be solved by control of building density in relation to transport facilities, and by curbing the crying evil of speculation in land values: elementary precautions which have been signally neglected in the United States. We have the inestimable advantage of initiating our own era of building upwards with a much truer understanding of the issues involved. That this form of construction has become inevitable in Europe is all the more reason for being thoroughly prepared for it. New York offers perfect cautionary examples of lack of foresight and what *not* to allow: dependence on artificial light throughout the day between the ground and fifteenth floors, and hundreds of millions of dollars sunk in tube railways that can never pay because they were built too late to serve their purpose. Practical experience alone can determine the most suitable mean height for European office-blocks, but structural and financial calculations have been worked out which seem to indicate that an eleven-storey type would probably prove to be the best.

The town—at once the embodiment of the corporate life of society and the symbol of its practical organization—gives us the clue whence that reforming impulse arose which led to the emergence of the New Architecture. A critical examination of existing urban conditions began to throw new light on their causes. It was realized that the present plight of our cities was due to an alarmingly rapid increase of the kind of functional maladies to which it is only in the natural order of things for all ageing bodies to be subject; and that these disorders urgently called for drastic surgical treatment. Yet the most important international congress of town-planners in recent years ended in impotent shrugging of shoulders because the assembled experts had to admit they commanded insufficient public support to enable them to apply the necessary remedies. The only resignation we can possibly indulge in is that of knowing we have no choice in the matter. Once the evils which produce the chaotic disorganization of our towns have been accurately diagnosed, and their endemic character demonstrated, we must see that they are permanently eradicated. The most propitious environment for propagating the New Architecture is obviously where a new way of thinking corresponding with it has already penetrated. It is only among intelligent professional and public-spirited circles that we can hope to arouse a determination to have done with the noxious anarchy of our towns. The technical means for carrying that determination into practical effect are already at our disposal. Had our civic mentality been sufficiently ripe to appreciate it we might now be reaping the benefit.

To sum up: the foundation of a flourishing modern school of architecture depends on the successful solution of a series of closely connected problems—the major issues of national planning, such as the readjustment of the relations between industry and agriculture and the redistribution of population on rational economic and geo-political principles; a re-orientation of town-planning, based on a progressive loosening of the city's tightly-woven tissue of streets by the alternation of rural and urban zones and a more organic concatenation of the residential and working districts with their educational and recreational centres; and, finally, the discovery of the ideal type of building. The intellectual groundwork of a new architecture is already established. What, metaphorically speaking, might be described as the bench-tests of its components have now been completed. There remains the task of imbuing the community with a consciousness of it and its essential rightness: a task which will devolve upon the uprising generation.

No one who has explored the sources of the movement I have called the New Architecture can possibly subscribe to the claim that it is based on an anti-traditional obsession for mechanistic technique *qua* mechanistic technique, which blindly seeks to destroy all deeper national loyalties and is doomed to lead to the deification of pure materialism. The laws by which it seeks to restrict arbitrary caprice are the fruit of a most thorough and conscientious series of investigations. In these I am proud to have taken a share. And I may add in parenthesis that I belong to a Prussian family of architects in which the tradition of Schinkel—the contemporary as well as the 'opposite number' of your own Soane—was part of our heritage. This in itself helps to convince me that my conception of the role of the New Architecture is nowhere and in no sense in opposition to 'Tradition' properly so-called. 'Respect for Tradition' does not mean the complacent toleration of elements which have been a matter of fortuitous chance or of individual eccentricity; nor does it mean the acceptance of domination by bygone aesthetic forms. It means, and always has meant, the preservation of essentials in the process of striving to get at what lies at the back of all materials and every technique, by giving semblance to the one with the intelligent aid of the other.

The ethical necessity of the New Architecture can no longer be called in doubt. And the proof of this—if proof were still needed—is that in all countries Youth has been fired with its inspiration.